a gift for:

from:

Nā
Wāhine

Nā
Wāhine

Hawaiian Proverbs and Inspirational Quotes
Celebrating Women in Hawai'i

Mutual Publishing

Library of Congress Catalog Card Number: 2003101068

ISBN 1-56647-596-1

Designed by Jane Hopkins

First Printing, May 2003
Second Printing, May 2004
2 3 4 5 6 7 8 9

Mutual Publishing
1215 Center Street, Suite 210
Honolulu, Hawai'i 96816
Ph: (808) 732-1709 / Fax: (808) 734-4094
e-mail: mutual@mutualpublishing.com / www.mutualpublishing.com

Printed in Korea

Introduction
by U'i Goldsberry

Women are the nurturing element of society, lending support and comfort to those in power and those powerless to defend themselves. In times of peace and war, they have lavished love and hope, and kindled the light of compassion.

All that is good in our world of diametric opposition is embodied in the abiding kindness and succor of women. All of the progress we have made as a species is directly attributed to the teaching and example of women. Their power is absolute, and their strength limitless.

The women of Hawai'i, through their cultural diversity and their collective spirit of optimism, personify the four elements of nature that have built and defined our Islands. They are fire, burning with the heat of the goddess Pele, fierce in the protection of their children, and smoldering in their passion. They are earth, grounding families with sensitivity and tradition, while giving birth and raising each consecutive generation. They are water, fluid in their movement, graceful in their determination. And they are air, boundless in their faith in the goodness of mankind.

Nā Wāhine, a book of celebration filled with song and proverb, portrait and quote, honors the women of Hawai'i nei. *"Me ke aloha no nā wāhine: nā kupunahine, nā mākuahine, me nā kaikamāhine o Hawai'i."* (With love to the women: the grandmothers, mothers, and daughters of Hawai'i.)

All that is Hawai'i is reflected in its women.

From Pele, the fiery goddess of the volcano,
to Laka, sensual goddess of the dance, to the
great earth mother Hinahina, to the powerful
chiefesses and queens, women have bound
this land together.

They are the earth, the essence.
They dazzle all with spirit, life, phosphorescence.
Their exuberance embraces everyone. Their
energy holds their families together. Every day,
they reveal hidden treasures: gold, fire,
and a core as hard as steel.

They have bound father to son with a caress.
They have suffused all with vibrations of
play, and dance. Their tears have washed away
pain, nourished, healed, and all they have
touched has become luminous.

Their strong hands have worked. Their
ancient shoulders have borne the children
of their womb, and the grief of centuries.

In the night, they have stood vigil over
those who sleep, are sick, have need. And at
dawn they have reached still deeper for that
hidden core of strength, banishing fear and
weariness with prayers and hope.

They have given birth. Washed. Dressed. Buried.
Renewed, refreshed, replenished.
Defied.

They are the common thread,
the golden thread that ties us together
and binds us to this land.

Diana Hansen-Young

E manaʻo aʻe ana e lei i ka lehua o Mokaulele.

A wish to wear the *lehua* of Mokaulele in *lei*.

A wish to win the maiden. *Lei* symbolizes sweetheart, and *lehua,* a pretty girl.

Nānā no a ka ʻulu i pakī kēpau.

Look for the gummy breadfruit.

Advice to a young girl—Look for a man who has
substance, like gummy breadfruit, which is
a sign of maturity.

Kūlia i ka nuʻu.

Strive to reach the highest.

Motto of Queen Kapiʻolani, 1834-1899

Aia nō ka pua i luna.

The flower is still on the tree.

A compliment to an elderly woman.
Her beauty still remains.

Without women there is no day and no night.

**Ang dalagang nagpopormal
sa kangyang kalagayan,
Hindi pagpapahamakan, ninum
angwalang pitagan.**

A woman who is dignified in her ways
is respected even by the irreverent.

Filipino proverb

**‘O ka papa he‘enalu kēia, pahe‘e
i ka nalu ha‘i o Makaiwa.**

This is the surfboard that will glide on the rolling surf of Makaiwa.

A woman's boast. Her beautiful body is like the surfboard on
which her mate "glides over the rolling surf."

A hahā, ua nani ka wahine la,
A hahā, ka nohona I ka laʻi
A hahā, ua hele a nohea la,
Pua haʻaheo o ke aupuni

Oh, oh, the girl is pretty,
Oh, oh, dwelling in peacefulness,
Oh, oh, so lovely,
Cherished flower of the nation.

Queen Liliʻuokalani
"He Inoa Nō Kaʻiulani"

He kai kapu ia na ke konohiki.

A forbidden beach reserved for the *konohiki*.

A maiden who is spoken for.

Hāʻawe i ke kua; hiʻi i ke alo.

A burden on the back; a babe in the arms.

Said of a hard-working woman who carries
a load on her back and a baby in her arms.

"Forth from her land to mine she goes,
The Island maid, the Island rose,
Light of heart and bright of face,
The daughter of a double race.
Her Islands here, in southern sun
Shall mourn their Ka'iulani gone,
And I, in dear banyan's shade,
Look vainly for the little maid.

But Scots Islands far away
Shall glitter with unwonted day,
And cast for once their tempest by
To smile in Ka'iulani's eye."

Robert Louis Stevenson

When a wife is beloved, the husband bows even
to a peg at her maiden home.

Korean proverb

**Na to tamahine ka pai i ta kina
mai ai teni ke keno ki konei.**

It was this lovely girl who brought the seal here.

Visits were often made by the sea, so the
beautiful young woman draws lovers to her as though
they were seals coming in from the sea.

Maori proverb

**The heart of a woman is as capricious as a drop
of water on a lotus leaf.**

Vietnamese proverb

Even when a girl is shy as a mouse, you still have to beware of the tiger within.

Chinese proverb

**A plain woman with moral beauty
is better than a beautiful woman.**

Vietnamese proverb

Though a beautiful woman does not say
anything, she cannot be hidden.

Japanese proverb

Huihui pāipu a Lono.

Lono's cluster of gourd vessels.

Lono was a woman who had a large family of children and an indolent, pleasure-seeking husband. Hers was a life of drudgery. Tired of it, she sought a home on the sun. But when she tried to go up to it, she grew so uncomfortably warm that she came down again. Then she tried to go to a star, but the twinkling of the stars made her feel that they were laughing at her plight. Then, when the full moon rose, she changed her children into gourds and traveled up a rainbow toward the moon. Her husband saw her and ran to grasp her ankle as she went up. Her foot slipped off like a lizard's tail. So Lono entered the moon and remained there. On full-moon nights, the people would point out the shadows in the moon and say, "There is Lono and her gourds." Today a mother who goes about with her flock of children is compared to Lono and her gourds.

"What is marriage, mother?"
"Child, it is spinning, having children, making money, and weeping."

Portuguese proverb

Oh, honest Americans,
as Christians hear me for my down-trodden
people! Their form of government is as dear to
them as yours is precious to you. Quite as
warmly as you love your country, so they love
theirs...It is for them that I would give the last
drop of my blood; it is for them that I would
spend, nay, am spending, everything belonging to
me. Will it be in vain? It is for the American
people and their representatives in Congress to
answer these questions. As they deal with me and
my people, kindly, generously and justly, so may
the Great Ruler of all nations deal with the
grand and glorious nation of the
United States of America.

Queen Lili'uokalani, 1896

Halakau ka manu i ka lāʻau.

The bird perches way up high in the tree.

Said of a woman who is not easily ensnared.

The most highly praised woman is the one about whom no one speaks.

Chinese proverb

...A majestic wahine with small,
bare feet, a grand, swinging, deliberate gait,
hibiscus blossoms in her flowing hair, and a lei of
yellow flowers flowing over her holoku, marching
through these streets, has a tragic grandeur of
appearance, which makes the diminutive,
fair-skinned haole, tottering along hesitatingly
in high-heeled shoes, look grotesque
by comparison.

Isabella Bird

He ʻiwa hoʻohaehae nāulu.

An *ʻiwa* that teases the rain clouds.

A beautiful maiden or handsome youth
who rouses jealous envy in others.

Out in Honolulu where the palm trees grow
lives a sweet Hawaiian maiden that loves me so
And when the moon is softly shining
We tell our stories all night long
listening to the music of the surf's wild roar
as it beats upon the golden shore...
She is my Rose of Honolulu,
she is my Hawaiian queen.

Beachboy Song

Luhi wahine ʻia.

Labored over by a woman.

Spoken in respect and admiration of a family
reared by a woman who alone fed and clothed them.

Look at the mother rather than her daughter.

In selecting a woman for your wife you should watch her mother
first in order to get some idea of the character of her daughter.

Japanese proverb

When I was born my mother gave me three names.
Christabelle, Yoshie, and Puanani.

Christabelle was my "english" name.
My social security name,
My school name,
    the name I gave when teachers asked me
    for my "real" name, a safe name.

Yoshie was my home name,
My everyday name,
    the name that reminded my father's family
    that I was Japanese, even though
    my nose, hips, and feet were wide,
    the name that made me acceptable to them
    who called my Hawaiian mother *kuroi* (black),
    a saving name.

Puanani is my chosen name,
My *piko* name connecting me to the *'āina*
    and the *kai* and the *po'e kahiko*
    my blessing; my burden,
    my amulet, my spear.

Puanani Burgess

A curious woman is capable of turning around
the rainbow just to see what is on the other side.

Chinese proverb

He ʻupena nae; ʻaʻohe iʻa hei ʻole.

It is a fine-meshed net;
there is no fish that it does not fail to catch.

Said of a woman who never fails to attract the opposite sex.

The native girls by twos and threes
and parties of a dozen, and sometimes in whole
platoons and companies, went cantering up and
down the neighboring streets astride of fleet but
homely horses, and with their gaudy riding
habits streaming like banners behind them. Such
a troop of free and easy riders, in their natural
home, which is the saddle, makes a gay
and graceful spectacle.

Mark Twain

Long as the lava light
Glares from the lava lake,
Dazing the starlight;
Long as the silvery vapor in daylight
Over the mountain
Floats, will the glory of Kapiolani be
mingled with either on Hawa-i-ee.

Alfred, Lord Tennyson,
glorifying Kapi'olani's defiance of Pele in 1824

Learning from my tūtū and aunty
meant being very disciplined; there was no
fooling around. You had to watch, listen and
follow. There wasn't a whole lot of in-depth
explanation of what you were doing. You
were expected to know it.

Hōkūlani Holt-Padilla

Ku i ka poholima ua mea he wahine maika'i.

A beautiful woman stands on the palm of the hand.

A beautiful woman makes one desire to caress and serve her.

One day at my grandparents', I was watching my grandmother quilting on the lānai while my grandfather raked leaves in the yard. My grandmother told me, "I don't hear the rake. Go to the railing and see what your grandfather is doing."

I saw him leaning on the rake, looking at a group of girls passing by. I reported this to my grandmother.

After a while, she went up behind him and said softly, "E nānā ana 'oe iā wai? Who are you looking at?"

Startled he said, "E nānā ana ho'i au, i ka māla pua e mā'alo ala." I was looking at a garden of flowers passing by.

Nana Veary

REFERENCES

Bird, Isabella L. *Six Months in the Sandwich Islands*. Honolulu: Mutual Publishing, 1998.

Chock, Eric and Harstad, James R. and Lum, Darrrell H.Y. and Teter, Bill eds. *Growing Up Local, An Anthology of Poetry and Prose from Hawai'i*. Honolulu: Bamboo Ridge Press, 1998.

de Ley, Gerd. *International Dictionary of Proverbs*. New York: Hippocrene Books, Inc, 1998.

Elbert, Samuel H. and Noelani Mahoe (collected by). "*He Inoa No Ka'iolani*" *by Queen Lili'uokalani, Na Mele o Hawai'i Nei*. Honolulu: The University of Hawaii Press, 1976.

Hansen-Young, Diana. *Sweet Paradise*. Honolulu: Mutual Publishing, 1986.

Itagaki, Jan M. and Lependu, Lovina, eds. *Nānā I Na Loea Hula, Look to the Hula Resources*. Honolulu: Kalihi-Pālama Culture & Arts Society, Inc, 1997

McGraw, Sister Martha Mary. *Stevenson in Hawaii*. Honolulu: University of Hawaii Press. 1950.

Meider, Wolfgang. *Illuminating Wit, Inspiring Wisdom, Proverbs from Around the World*. New Jersey: Prentice Hall Press, 1998.

Pukui, Mary Kawena. *'Olelo No'eau: Hawaiian Proverbs and Poetical Sayings*. Honolulu: Bishop Museum Special Publication No. 71, 1983.

Riley, Murdoch (compiled by). *Maori Sayings and Proverbs*. Paraparaumu N.Z.: Viking Sevenseas, 1990.

Timmons, Grady. *Waikiki Beachboy*. Honolulu: Editions Limited, 1989.

Veary, Nana. *Change We Must*. Honolulu: Institute of Zen Studies, 1989.

PHOTO CREDITS

Page 2: Mrs. Kuhihewa Kane, 1920-1921, Maui. Sullivan Collection, Bishop Museum.

Page 5: Hawai'i State Archives.

Page 7: Bishop Museum.

Page 10: Mrs. Kakuole Harbottle and Mrs. Kupukaa (sisters), 1920-1921, Kohala. Sullivan Collection. Bishop Museum.

Page 11: Craig T. Kojima, Star-Bulletin.

Page 13: old postcard image.

Page 15: Selling mangoes, Lahaina. Ray Jerome Baker, Bishop Museum.

Page 17: Queen Kapi'olani in her coronation robes, 1883. Baker-Van Dyke Collection.

Page 19: Mrs. Kaluna Linsey, 1920-1921, Kamuela. Sullivan Collection, Bishop Museum.

Page 21: Unidentified woman, standing. Usaku Tergawachi, Bishop Museum.

Page 23: Hawai'i State Archives.

Page 25: Baker-Van Dyke Collection.

Page 27: Princess Ka'iulani. Hawai'i State Archives.

Page 29: Baker-Van Dyke Collection.

Page 31: Interior of Hawaiian home with two women holding babies, ca. 1890. Bishop Museum.

Page 33: Princess Ka'iulani as a teenager. Hawai'i State Archives.